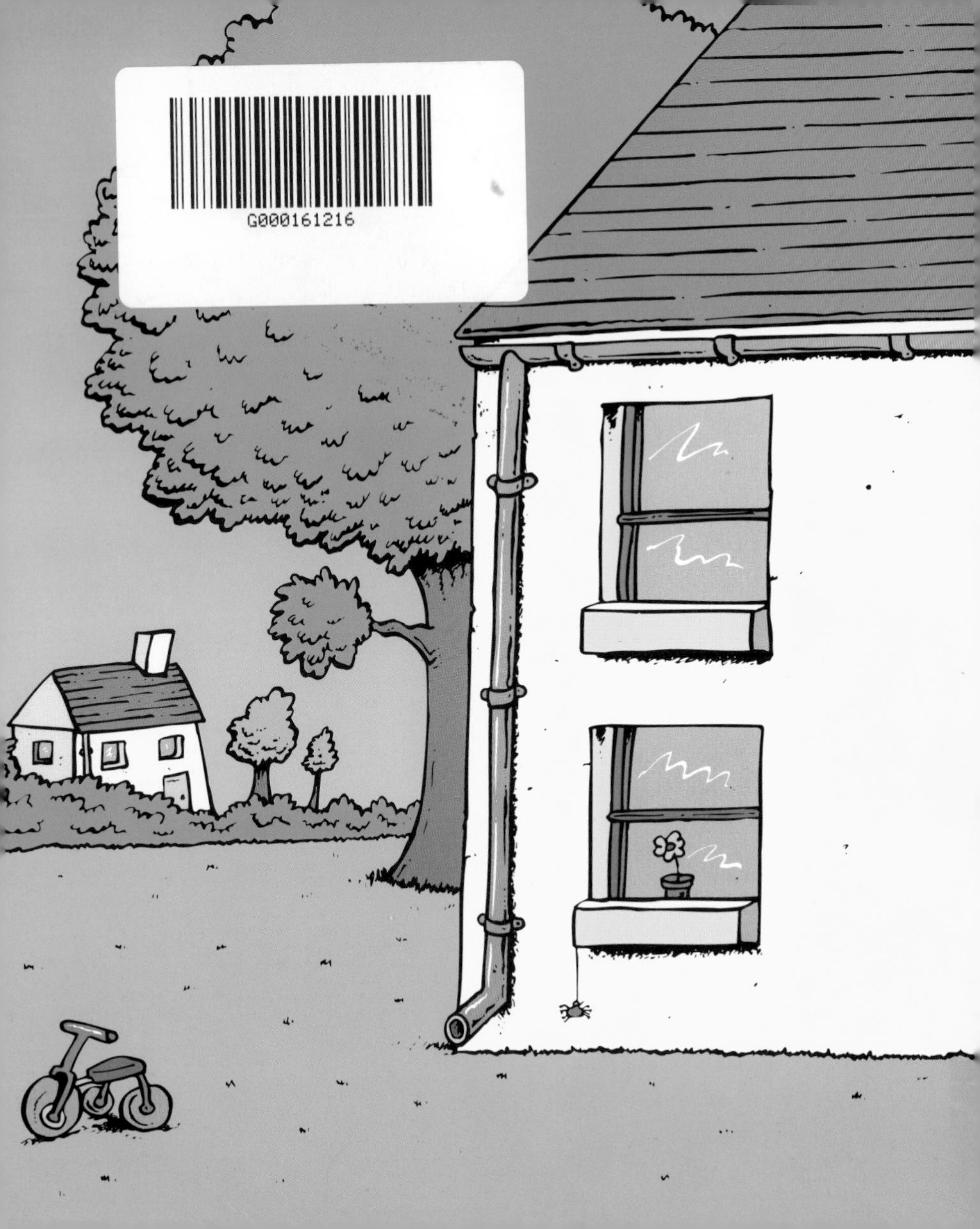

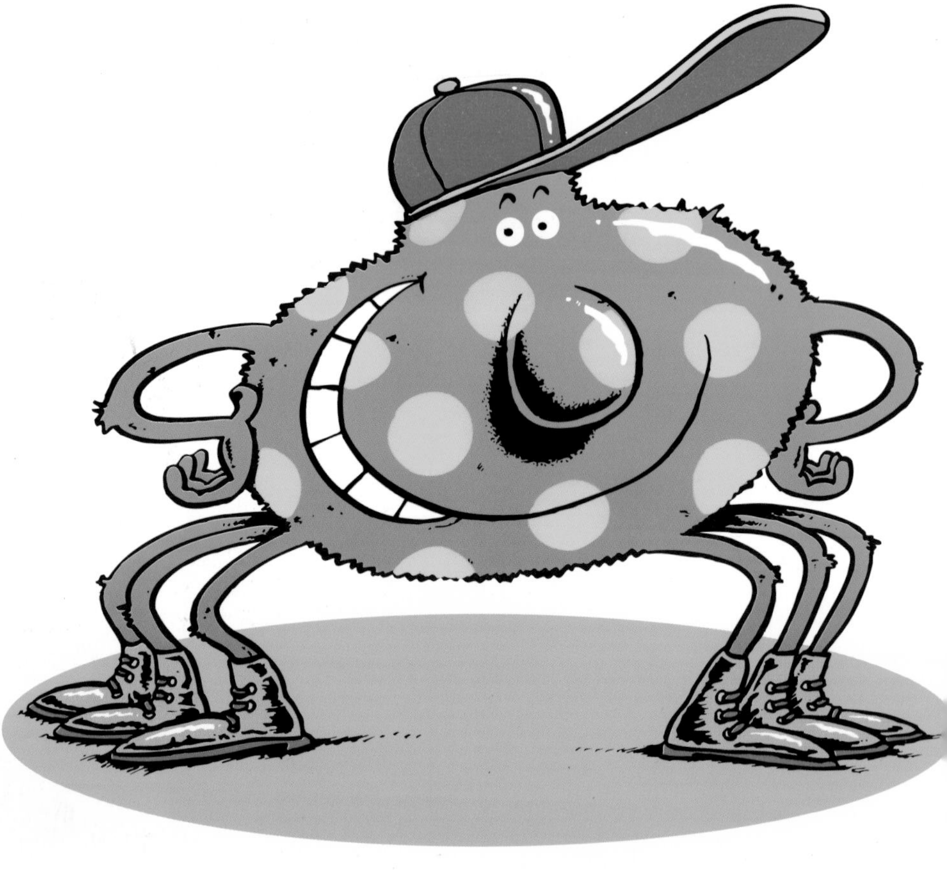

Incy Wincy Spider

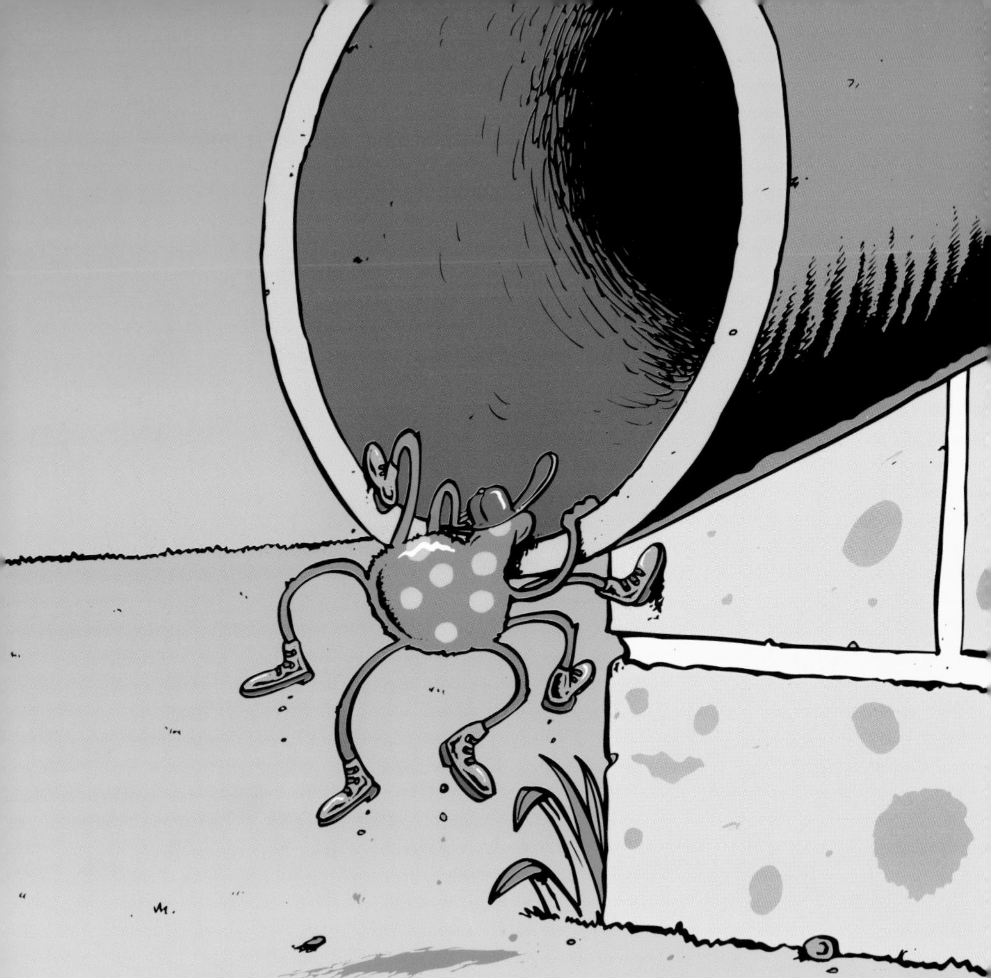

climbed up the water spout.

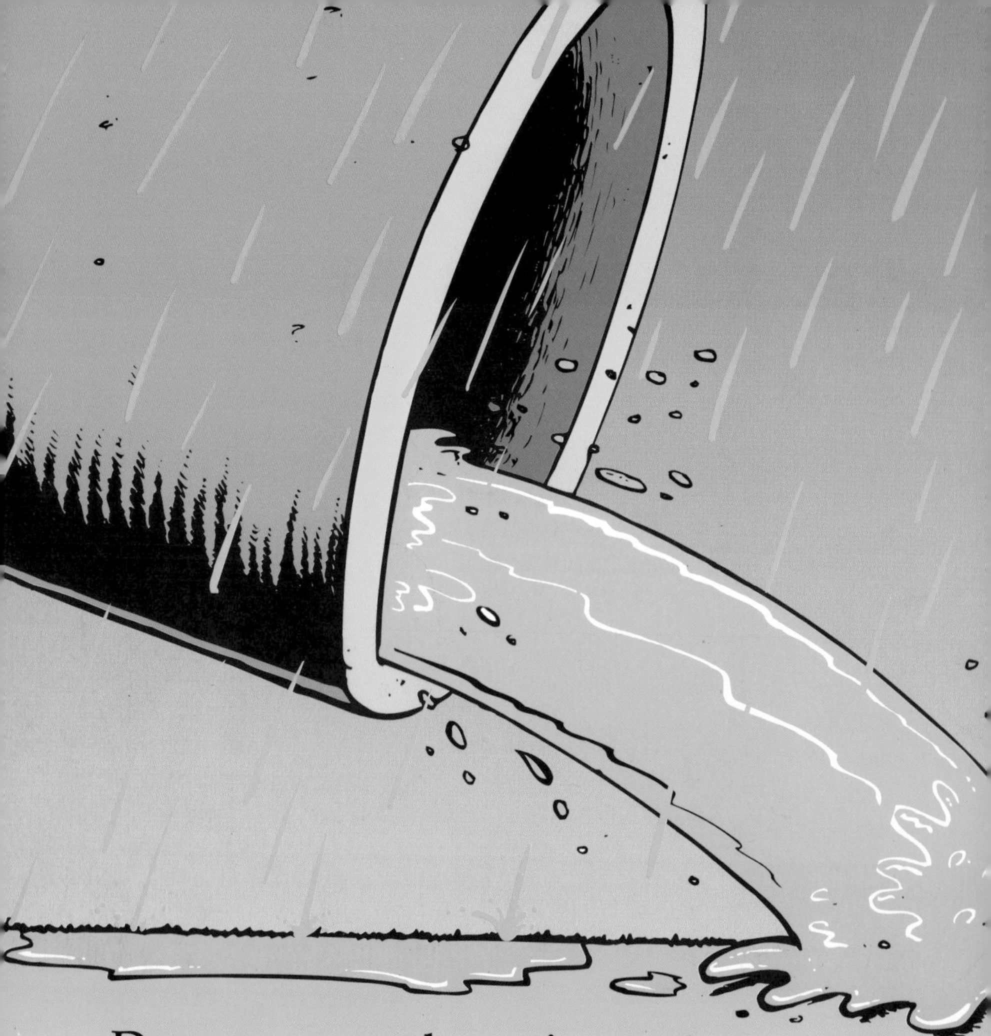

Down came the rain and

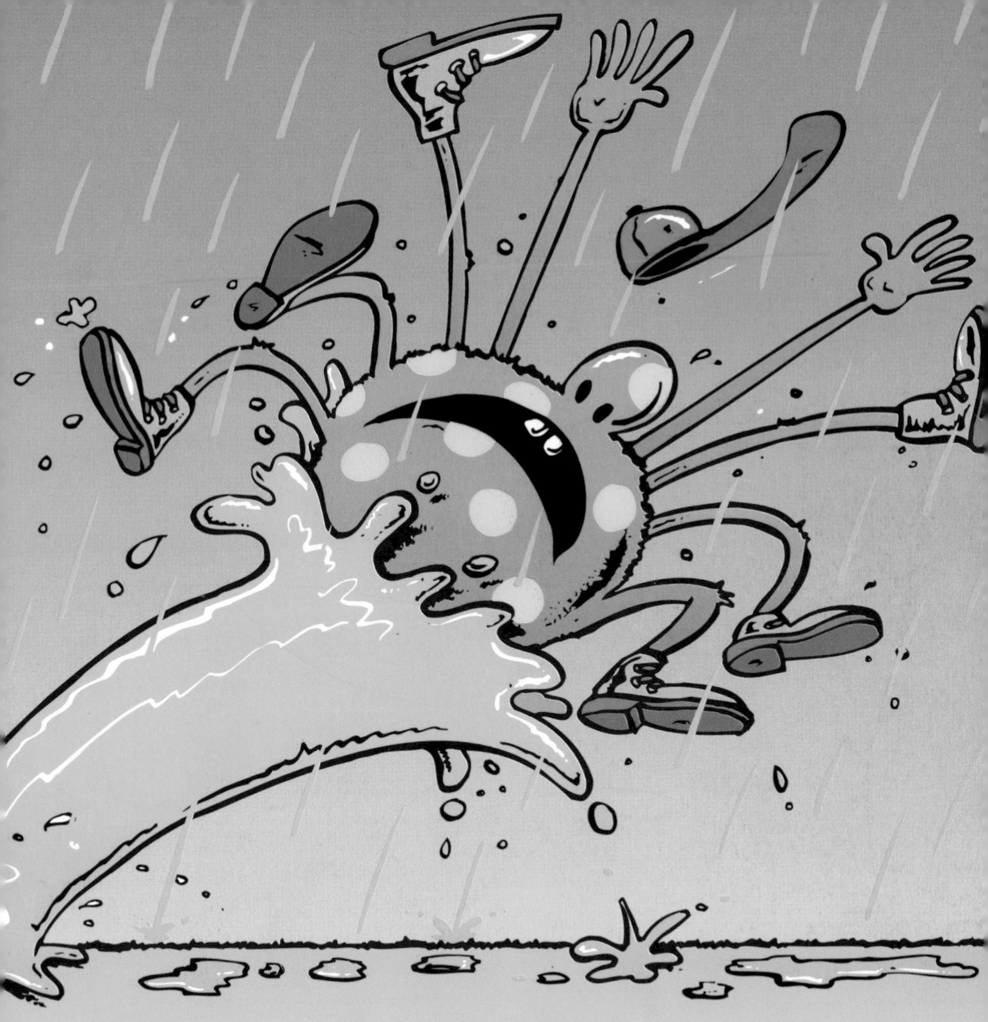

washed poor Incy out.

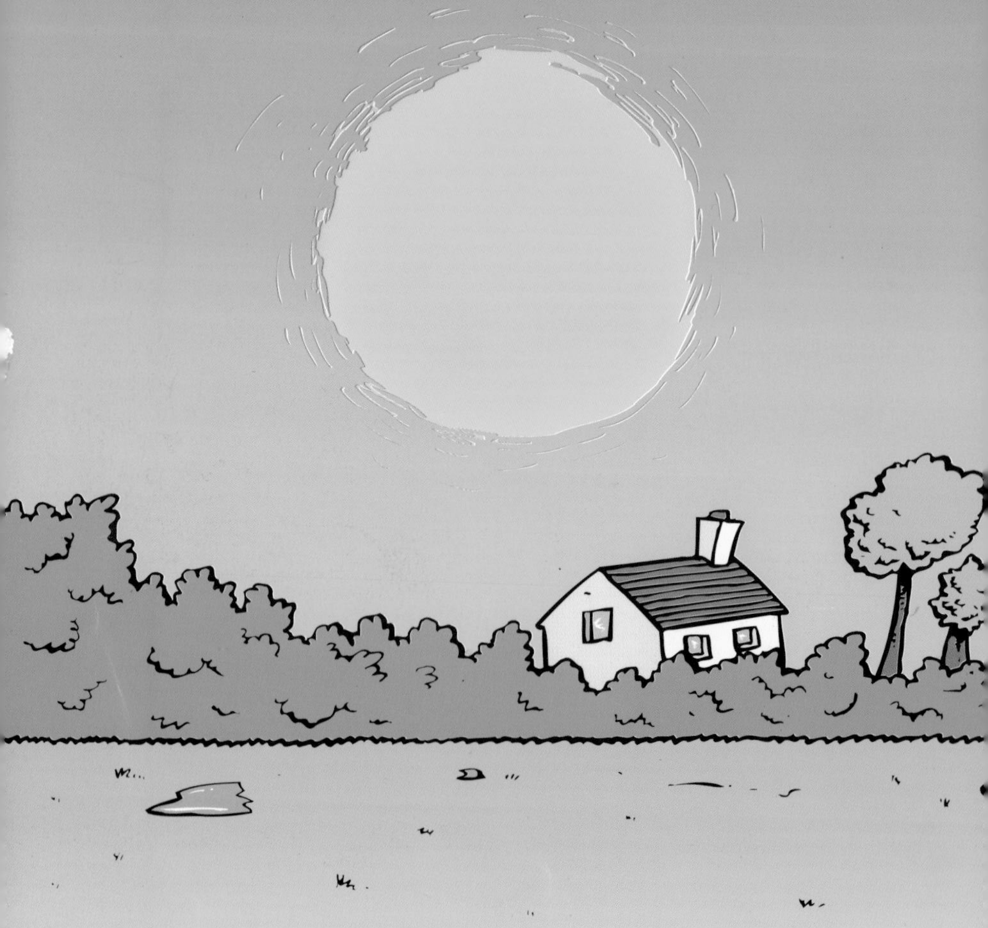

Out came the sun and

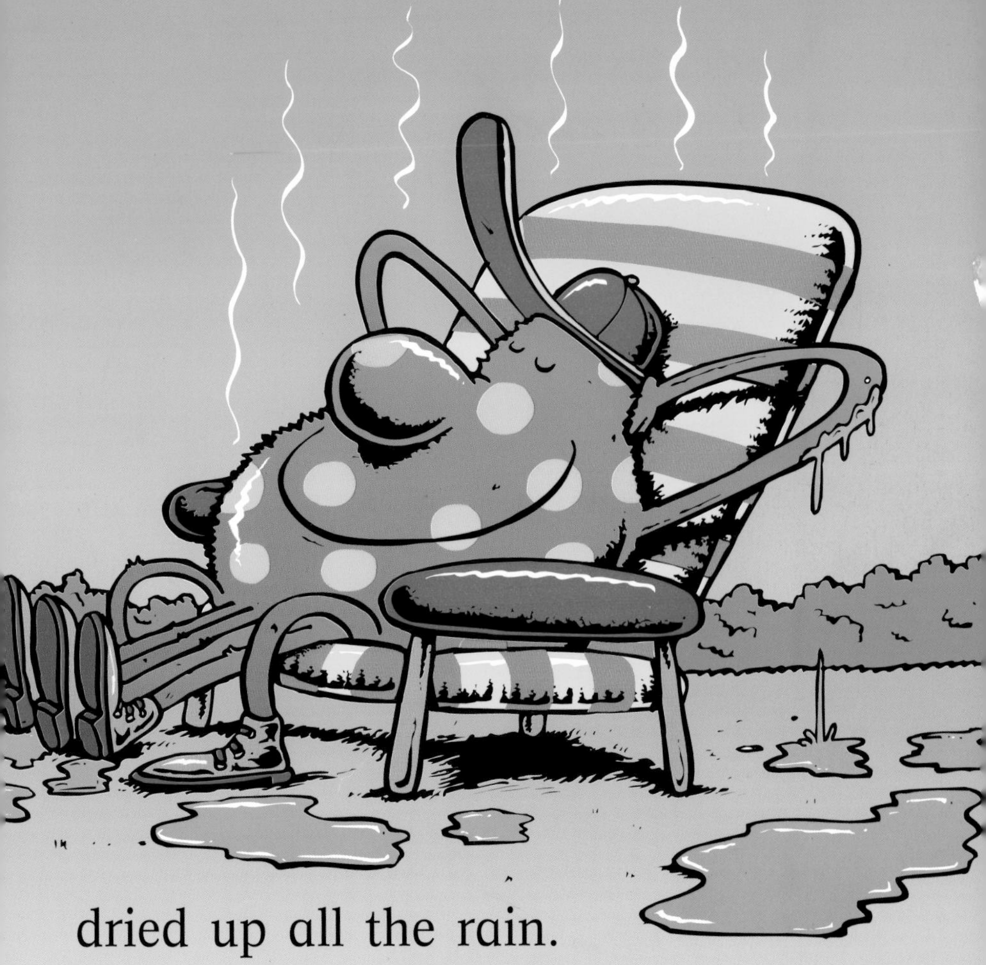

dried up all the rain.

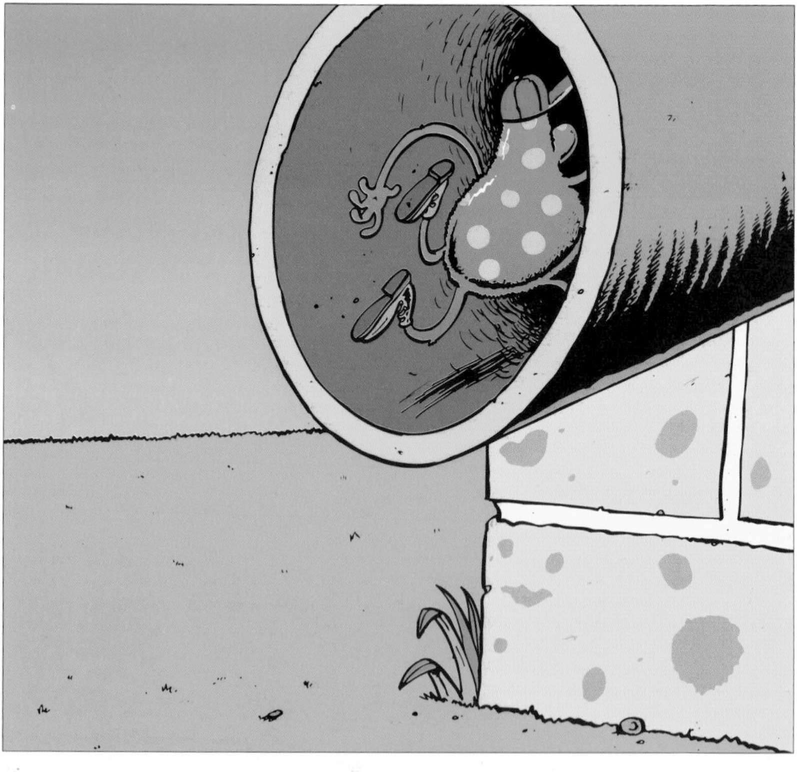

So Incy Wincy Spider
climbed up the spout again.